I0168875

William Penniman Clarke

A base slander refuted

Vol. 1

William Penniman Clarke

A base slander refuted
Vol. 1

ISBN/EAN: 9783337884895

Printed in Europe, USA, Canada, Australia, Japan

Cover: Foto ©ninafisch / pixelio.de

More available books at **www.hansebooks.com**

[From the Daily Morning Chronicle, Washington City, D. C., December 27th.]

A BASE SLANDER REFUTED.

WE print to-day a long communication from W. Penn. Clarke, Esq., formerly chief clerk of the Interior Department, under Secretary Harlan, defending the latter from an attack on his character as a public officer and a good citizen by a correspondent of the Cincinnati *Gazette.* No one who reads Mr. Clarke's communication can for a moment doubt that Mr. Harlan has been wantonly and wickedly assailed, and that the charges brought against him are utterly baseless.

To the Editor of the Chronicle:

The Washington correspondent of the Cincinnati *Daily Gazette,* of the 17th inst., referring to the pending Senatorial contest in Iowa, and apparently for the purpose of damaging the prospects of some of the gentlemen whose names are being used in that connection, travels out of his way to assail the character of ex-Secretary Harlan, now one of the oldest and most distinguished members of the United States Senate. In relation to the *animus* of the writer, it may be observed that it is susceptible of proof that he has admitted that his chief grievance was a supposed sympathy of the ex-Secretary with General O. O. Howard in a church controversy between that one armed veteran of the recent war and the correspondent's father, an ex chaplain of the House of Representatives, and which resulted in dividing the Congregational Church of this city. It has also now become public, as a piece of city gossip, that this correspondent (and perhaps some other correspondents of the public press) has taken offense at Senator Harlan and his family, on account of some supposed indignity which he imagines he had suffered, or some discrimination in favor of one of the reporters for the CHRONICLE, at the time of the marriage of the Secretary's daughter to Robert T. Lincoln, son of the late President—he and they not being informed of the fact that Mr. Lincoln had requested that the wedding should be as private as practicable, on account of his mother, who very naturally wished to be present, and who was still in mourning over the terrible death of her illustrious husband. Your reporter was at the time temporarily connected with one of Mr. Harlan's Senate committees, and consequently regarded as a member of his official household—a fact that was probably overlooked by the *Gazette* correspondent and others to whom we have alluded. These seem to be, and so far as is known, are, the motives which have led to this malevolent assault upon the character of one of the most distinguished of our Republican Senators, which is more disgraceful to the author than the gentleman whom he has assailed, and which cannot but excite the condemnation of all right-thinking men.

One other motive may have contributed to this attack. The tone and temper of this *Gazette* letter would seem to justify the conviction that it may have been inspired, to some extent, by the over-anxious friends of some aspirant for senatorial honors in Iowa, whose interests it was imagined might be advanced by blighting the fair fame of those who were considered obstacles in the way of success. But this of itself would hardly be a sufficient motive, for we have reason to believe that Senator Harlan has taken no part in the contest, nor even expressed a preference in favor of any one of the various aspirants.

The charges against the ex-Secretary are not only malevolent, but contemptible in their character. Nearly all of the allegations of misconduct relate to trivial matters, out of which, according to the writer's own showing, it would have been impossible to realize sufficient pecuniary profit to amount to *a temptation* to do wrong on the part of a high official of the Government. If the head of a Department, who controls the disbursement of multiplied millions of the public treasure were disposed to defraud the Government, he would hardly waste his time in an attempt to misapply a few quires of paper, or a few tons of coal. The charges, therefore, are not only improbable in themselves, but are contradicted by the whole tenor of Senator Harlan's public and private life and character. Upon these he might safely rely as a complete defense against the envenomed attacks of anonymous sensational writers, and not fear the result. But in justice to Senator Harlan, and as a duty we owe to the party organization of which he is one of the oldest and most useful members, we shall proceed to *refute* the charges of the *Gazette* correspondent, and demonstrate that they are destitute of any foundation in fact or truth.

Dr. John R. Goodwin is our first witness—the very man whom the *Gazette* correspondent insinuates knows all the facts. While Mr. Harlan was Secretary of the Interior, Goodwin was the disbursing officer of the Department, as he is at the present time; and in the following affidavit he thus sums up and contradicts many of the charges of the *Gazette:*

WASHINGTON, D. C, Dec 23, 1869.

In a communication published in the *Cincinnati Daily Gazette* of the 17th inst., the writer assails the character of the Hon. James Harlan, by charging: that while Secretary of the Interior, he appointed his son to the office of messenger; that he used Government horses, and paid $60 per month for keeping the pair; that he paid the driver of the team from the public funds; that he discharged the driver because he refused to dress in livery, at his own expense; that he caused a bill of $650 for fancy paper, cards, knives, scissors, &c, for the use of his household, to be paid for from the contingent fund of the Department; that he caused coal to be sent from the cellars of the Department to his own house, for his private use; that he rented, and caused to be fitted up, rooms for my private use, with public funds; and that he took carpets and other articles from the Department, and converted them to private use

I. on oath, say that during the greater part of the time that Mr. Harlan was Secretary of the Interior I was disbursing clerk and superintendent of the building. During that time, I paid all bills that were paid for salaries and for contingencies, and also, as superintendent, had charge of the purchase of stationery, and furniture, and fuel for the Department; and the contracts and bills connected with such purchases are now in the office of the disbursing clerk. These show that the Secretary's son was paid as a messenger for the period of seventy-three (73) days, and no more; during that time he performed duty as messenger, often during the day, and often at night The rate of pay was that usually paid to messengers, and allowed by law.

Every member of the Cabinet has a span of horses furnished and boarded for official use, and also a driver. Mr. Harlan paid $50 per month for the board, and not $60, as alleged. This is the record, and it is the customary price.

Mr Harlan's driver never dressed in livery. I am of opinion that he never discharged a driver because he would not dress in livery, else the successor would have so dressed.

He never caused to be paid $720 each, on the rolls of the Department, to two men—one for a footman, and one for a dining-room servant. I am intimately acquainted with Mr. Harlan and his family, and was frequently at his house as a personal friend while he was Secretary, and personally know that he had a sufficient number of private servants to perform all the ordinary duties connected with his household.

I have carefully examined the records of the office, and find no bill of $650 as having been paid for fancy stationery, &c., for the use of his household nor any other that can justify the charge. There was no such bill paid.

He never rented any room for my private use During his term of service I occupied rooms rented by myself from Mr. Samuel Magee, an old citizen, and the Government never paid for any rooms occupied by myself for private use.

He never received from the cellars of the Department any coal for his private use. If such had been the case, I, as superintendent, would have known it

He never received from the Department carpets or other furniture which he did not pay for at a full value, appraised by impartial and competent appraisers. JOHN R. GOODWIN.

District of Columbia, Washington County to wit:

On this 24th day of December, 1869, before me, one of the justices of the peace in and for said county, personally appeared John R. Goodwin, who, upon being sworn according to law, did depose and say that the foregoing statement is true and correct in every particular.

Subscribed and sworn to before me on this day.
[SEAL.] R. B. NIXON, J. P.

Thomas D. Bond, then as now, Chief Engineer of the Interior Department, and the custodian of the fuel of the Department, makes the following statement under oath, which, in connection with the affidavit of Dr. Goodwin, completely disposes of the dastardly slander about the misuse of government coal:

I, Thomas D. Bond, on oath, depose and say, that I am now, and was during the whole period of Hon. James Harlan's service as Secretary of the Interior, Chief Engineer of said Department, and was then, and am now, custodian of all the fuel received for its use; and I further depose and say, that I know [personally that no coal or other fuel was ever taken from the Department to the residence of the said Secretary. I also depose and say, that I acted as the said Secretary's agent in purchasing fuel for his residence and office at his house; that several times I procured it of the government contractor, but that in every case, a separate bill was made out against the Secretary for the whole amount, and paid for by me as his agent, he handing me the money to pay for the same; and that no part of said coal or other fuel was ever paid for by the Department. I also depose and say, that I was intimately acquainted with said Secretary and his family, was often in and through his house, and do not believe it possible that property of any kind could have been taken from the Department to, and used at, his residence, without my knowledge; and that he was always scrupulously exact in paying for every thing, even of the most trivial character, turned over to his private use or that of his family.

THOMAS D. BOND.

District of Columbia, Washington County, to wit:

On this 21st day of December, 1869, before me, the subscriber, one of the justices of the peace in and for said county, personally appeared Thomas D. Bond, and being sworn according to law, did depose and say that the within statement is true and correct.

Subscribed and sworn to before me this 21st day of December, 1869.
[SEAL.] R. B. NIXON, J. P.

The next charge against the ex-Secretary is, that he became the purchaser of a pair of horses belonging to the Department at a nominal value. This falsehood is completely refuted by the following affidavit of Charles H. Sherrill, John T. Price, and Colonel Theodore B. Samo, all three well known gentlemen of this city, of unimpeachable character, and known to be excellent judges of this kind of property. Colonel Samo was then, and is now, in the service of the Interior Department as the engineer of the aqueduct, and Mr. Price is an old and large dealer in horses, and well known to all dealers in stock. But to the affidavit:

WASHINGTON CITY, D C., Dec. 24, 1869.

The undersigned, Charles H. Sherrill, John T. Price, and Theodore B. Samo, having seen an article published in the Cincinnati Gazette of the 17th instant, charging Hon. James Harlan with having procured a couple of horses of the Interior Department at a nominal price, state on oath, that on the request of the Secretary, we examined and appraised said horses before their purchase, and valued one of them at one hundred dollars, and the other one at two hundred dollars. The first one was old, and was afflicted with the disease known as heaves; the other was defective, being knee-sprung and afflicted with corns and other defects No one of us thought the horses worth more than the price named, and some thought them worth less than the amount named; and no one of us then thought that they would have commanded that price in open market. We were each well acquainted with said horses. Two of us had often driven them, and the other one of us, John T Price, is, and has been for a long period, a dealer in horses; and we consider ourselves good judges of the value of that kind of stock.

CHAS H. SHERRILL,
JOHN T PRICE,
THEODORE B. SAMO.

District of Columbia, Washington County, to wit:

On this 24th day of December, 1866, before me, one of the justices of the peace in and for the said county, personally appeared Charles H. Sherrill, John T. Price, and Theodore B Samo, who being each and severally sworn according to law, did depose and say that the within statement was true and correct.

Subscribed and sworn to before me this day,

[SEAL]   R B NIXON, J. P.

The truth about this whole horse matter is that Senator Harlan's family, having occasionally used the horses, and became attached to them, desired to retain them, and he, to gratify the family, purchased the horses at more than their real cash value. No one can doubt this after reading the foregoing affidavit. We might rest the refutation of these charges in relation to the coal and horses upon the sworn statements of the gentlemen above named, but to leave no room for doubt that all these things were honestly paid for, we annex the following receipts:

Received, Washington, D. C., August 31, 1866, of Hon James Harlan, $320 for one pair of horses and harness, as per appraisement.

WILLIAM S. MARSH,
Disbursing Agent, (Aqueduct.)

WASHINGTON, D. C., August 9, 1866.

HON JAMES HARLAN Bought of S. P. BROWN & SON, forwarding and commission merchants, No. 456 Ninth street between L and F streets:

1866—August 9 10 tons L. M, white ash egg coal at $7 90 .... $79 00
1866—August 9 11 tons red ash stove at $8 10 89 10
                                              168 10

Received payment,
[Stamp]   S. P. BROWN & SON.

WASHINGTON, January 18, 1866.

HON. JAMES HARLAN
To H. CLAY STEWART, Dr
1865—Dec. 14. To 5 tons grate coal at $9 40.. $47 10
        5 tons furnace do., at $9 90. 49 50
        Putting in do , 10 tons, at
        75 cents 7 50
1866—Jan. 18. To 10 tons coal at $15........ 150 00
        Putting in 10 tons at 75c..   7 50
                                       261 60

Received payment,
[Stamp]   H CLAY STEWART.

Now, in relation to the charge about the furniture. It has been the custom from the formation of the Department for the Government to furnish a room at the Secretary's residence for an office, where he receives visitors, and often transacts public business after office hours. This was done in Secretary Harlan's case as a matter of course, including desk, carpet, office chairs, &c. While this was being done, some pieces of first-class off carpeting, considered worthless, were procured by his family for the use of the domestics in the kitchen and basement; and, at or about the time of Secretary Harlan's retirement from the Department, all of these articles at his request, were appraised, and subsequently paid for by him, as is shown by the following receipt:

DEPARTMENT OF THE INTERIOR.
WASHINGTON, December 1, 1866.

Received of Hon. James Harlan, two hundred and ninety-five dollars, ($295) to pay for furniture,

&c, as per appraisement of Mr. E H King, made December 1, 1866, and on file in the Department of the Interior.   J R. GOODWIN,
Superintendent.

We come next to the ridiculous statement in relation to services of Department employees at Mr. Harlan's residence. Mr. William Syphax has been, almost since the organization of the Interior Department, the messenger of the Secretary, and still holds that position. It is his duty to take in to the Secretary the cards of visitors, and usher them into his presence. By reason of this long service, he has become personally acquainted with all the Senators and members of Congress, as well as other officials; and on public occasions, as he states in the following affidavit, he frequently attended at Mr. Harlan's to attend the door and receive the visitors, for which service he was always generously paid by the Senator's lady. If any of the other employees rendered any services at the residence of the Senator, it was usually on similar occasions, when they were not required to be at the Department, and for which they were amply compensated. The charge that the Secretary's servants wore livery, and that the coachman was discharged for the reason that he refused to purchase a suit of livery at his own expense, is refuted by the statements of Dr. Goodwin given above. The affidavit of Mr. Syphax reads as follows:

WASHINGTON, D. C., December 14, 1869.

I, William Syphax, on oath, state that I am now, and was during the whole period of Hon. James Harlan's service as Secretary of the Interior, and for a long period before, messenger to the Secretary; that I was familiarly acquainted with Secretary Harlan's household, and that, on extraordinary occasions such as public receptions, during what is called the fashionable season, when there were multitudes of official callers and visitors, I was frequently at his house (as I know personally nearly all the Senators and members and other high officials,) to attend the door and receive the guests, as was the custom before he became Secretary, and that I rendered such service voluntarily, at or office hours, and was always well paid therefor by Mrs. Harlan.

W. SYPHAX.

District of Columbia, Washington County, to wit:

On this 24th day of December, 1869, before me, one of the justices of the peace in and for the said county, personally appeared William Syphax, who being sworn according to law, did depose and say that the foregoing statement is true and correct.

Subscribed and sworn to before me this day.

[SEAL]   R B NIXON, J. P.

The following affidavit of Judge Killpatrick is also to the same purport:

WASHINGTON, December 25, 1869.

I, Ephraim Killpatrick, state on oath that during the whole time that Hon. James Harlan was secretary of the Interior I was a clerk in the Department, part of the time acting as chief clerk, and the remainder of the time as a clerk in in one of the divisions of the office, the most of the time at a desk in the room occupied by the Secretary; that I was intimately acquainted with the Secretary and his family, and was often at his house; his family consisted of himself, his wife, and two children; that he had at his house continuously several servants—enough in my judgment, to perform all the ordinary duties connected with his household—in no way connected with the Department, or borne on its rolls. He had a room fitted up as an office at his residence, as I understand has always been the custom of the head of the Department, where he transacted a large amount of official business, and I have observed an employee—sometimes one and sometimes another—at this office room, to attend at the door and to do messenger duty, and I have been told that said employe sometimes exchanged work with one of the private servants. On public occasions, such as receptions, dinners, and during what is called the fashionable season, and periods of extraordinary pressure, when there was a multitude of official callers, messengers and other employes of the Department were frequently present, rendering the necessary assistance; but, as far as I ever noticed, none of the Department messengers or employes were ever so employed as to interfere with their official duties. I further state that Mr. Harlan, so far as I know and believe, has never, either while he was Secretary, or before or since, had a servant in livery in his employ, either as coachman or in any other capacity.

E. KILLPATRICK.

District of Columbia, Washington County, to wit:

On this 26th day of December, 1869, before the subscriber, one of the justices of the peace in and for the said county, personally appeared E. Killpatrick, who, being sworn according to law, did depose and say that the foregoing statement is true and correct in every particular.

Subscribed and sworn to before me.

[SEAL.] R. B. NIXON, J. P.

Having disposed of these trivial charges against the ex-Secretary—and which we have shown to be the mere inventions of a malicious heart—we proceed to notice others more particularly affecting his official conduct, and which will be found equally unsupported by truth. The unblushing declaration that Secretary Harlan violated the law in accepting the first section of forty miles of the Kansas branch of the Union Pacific Railroad, and the cowardly insinuation that he did so from improper considerations received from the company, through its President, John D Perry, is driven to the wall by the voluntary statement of General William J Palmer, the Treasurer of the company, sent to Mr. Harlan last winter, after that gentleman had read a similar attack in the *Gazette*, made by this same correspondent, about a year since. From this statement it appears that Secretary Harlan was overruled by the then President, Andrew Johnson, and afterwards acted in this matter under the President's orders:

UNION PACIFIC RAILWAY, E. D.,
WASHINGTON, D. C., February 28, 1869

Hon James Harlan, U. S. Senator:

SIR: My attention having been called to a publication in the Cincinnati *Gazette* of the 23d ult., charging you with dereliction of duty as Secretary, in connection with the acceptance of the first section of forty miles of the Union Pacific railway, eastern division, and particularly noting an apparent conflict between your recommendation of May 29, 1866, advising the President that said section should not be accepted, and your letter of October 23, 1866, following, in which, after reciting that the company had entered into an agreement to make certain required improvements, you advised that the Secretary of the Treasury and the Secretary of the Interior be directed to carry into effect the provisions of law in regard to said completed section, I deem it due to you, and to truth, to say that I was at the time personally present at interviews between yourself and officers of said company, and between said officers and the President of the United States; that a difference of opinion arose between you and the company in regard to the degree of perfection required by the law under the phrase, "first-class railroad;" that you uniformly and persistently insisted on a higher standard being adopted than that set up by the company and the commissioners first appointed to examine said road; that you frankly told the officers of the company that, so far as it depended on your official action neither the bonds nor the lands pertaining to said section would be issued and patented until said section was made to conform to a standard higher than that which the company thought

the law required, or that was practicable under the limited aid granted by the Government in that new country.

Deeming it to be the province of the President of the United States, and not that of the Secretary of the Interior, to decide whether the said section had or had not been constructed according to law, the officers of the company requested him to examine the subject personally, which he proceeded to do; whereupon a full and free conference was had at the Executive Mansion, between the President, the Secretary of the Interior, the Secretary of the Treasury, the officers of the Company, and several of the principal stockholders of the road, where every thing pertaining to said section of road was fully explained, and all objections to its acceptance were fully canvassed. This interview resulted as we expected, in an executive order for the issuance of the subsidy in bonds and lands, pertaining to said section, the company first agreeing to make certain improvements of grades, curves, bridges, &c, which their own and the public interest demanded, and which they contemplated making had no such agreement been entered into.

It is perhaps proper that I should also state that I was at that time, and have been ever since, Treasurer of said company, and have been the custodian of its books and papers, and that I personally know that you have never had at any time the slightest pecuniary interest in this company, its property, or franchises.

Very respectfully, your obedient servant,
WM. J. PALMER.

The malicious character of this attack on Senator Harlan is further evidenced by the reproduction by this correspondent of his old charge in relation to the sale of the Cherokee neutral lands, and needs no other notice than the statement that this slander was completely exposed and refuted by Mr. Harlan on the floor of the Senate last winter, and that the public records show that the sale made by him was at as high a rate as the land would at that time bring in the market; and that after ample advertising, and delaying the sale for more than a year, his successor, Hon. O. H. Browning, was unable to effect a sale at a higher rate. These facts are established by House Ex. Doc. No. 85, 2d session Fortieth Congress, over Mr. Browning's own signature, from which we extract the following

In respect to the sale of the Cherokee neutral lands I deem it proper to remark that by the terms of the treaty it is optional with the Secretary of the Interior to sell them in separate tracts at not less than an average of $1 25 per acre, or in a body at not less than $1 per acre.

The provision of the treaty for the sale in separate tracts is, that after the lands shall have been surveyed, they shall be appraised at an average of not less than $1 25 per acre, exclusive of improvements, and after advertising for sealed bids, shall be sold to the highest bidder, for cash, in parcels not exceeding one hundred and sixty acres, and at not less than the appraised value.

Another provision of the treaty authorizes the Secretary of the Interior to sell the whole of said lands not occupied by actual settlers, in a body, to any responsible party, for cash, for a sum not less than $1 per acre.

The sale in separate parcels, on sealed bids, is subject to the disadvantages of requiring years of time and of leaving all the refuse lands in the hands of the Indians unsold. I did not doubt that an immediate sale, in a body, at $1 per acre, would be greatly more to the interest of the Indians than a tardy sale of the choice lands in separate tracts at the appraised value, with the inferior lands left undisposed of for years, and have, consequently, been desirous to find a purchaser who would take them all, good and bad together, at $1 per acre.

With this view I suggested and urged at the last session of Congress that the United States should become the purchaser, at one dollar per acre, and issue bonds in payment thereof. Such a proposition was, I believe, submitted to Congress, but not accepted.

After the adjournment of Congress I authorized an unofficial statement to be made to the news papers that the proposals for the purchase of said lands in a body would be received at the Department until the 1st of October.

Early in October Mr. James F. Joy, of Detroit, Mich., proposed to take the lands in a body at one dollar per acre, and pay the cash for them.

No other offer was made; I accepted Mr. Joy's, and concluded a contract with him, from which all lands occupied by actual settlers at the date of the ratification of the treaty were excluded. A copy of the contract is herewith furnished.

The money would have been paid by Mr. Joy, and the lands conveyed at the time of the contract, had the number of acres sold been known. But as all the lands occupied by actual settlers were excluded from the sale, it was necessary to ascertain the quantity thus occupied to determine how many acres remained to be paid for by Mr. Joy. Commissioners are now engaged in estimating and appraising the improved tracts. As soon as they shall have completed their labors and reported, the contract will be consummated by accepting the purchase money and causing the land to be patented to the purchaser.

Very respectfully, your obedient servant,
O. H. BROWNING, Secretary.

HON. SCHUYLER COLFAX, Speaker of the House of Representatives

That this subsequent sale by Mr. Browning was not considered by the Indians the Department, and the Senate, more for the interest of the Cherokee tribe, than the sale previously made by Mr. Harlan, is fully proved by the fact that a subsequent treaty was made between the Cherokees and the Government, which was ratified by the Senate, authorizing the cancellation of the sale made by Secretary Browning, and *carrying into effect that previously made by Secretary Harlan*. It may not be improper to add, in this connection, as showing the confidence in Senator Harlan's integrity entertained by his brother Senators, that in the face of this slander, and while it must have been fresh in the memory of each, the Senate placed that gentleman at the head of the Committee of Indian Affairs, where he still remains, thus evidencing their appreciation of his knowledge of the subjects pertaining to that committee, and their undiminished respect for him as an upright man.

The last allegation contained in this correspondent's letter, affecting Mr. Harlan's character, charges that he and Commissioner Cooley, of the Indian Bureau, "worked night and day to perfect a sale of the Delaware Indian lands, on fraudulent papers of so transparent a character that a clerk, who was directed by Cooley to fill them up, thrust them back in his face, telling him plainly that the whole thing was a swindle, which would return one day to damn all connected with it But the matter was driven through by the active and combined efforts of Harlan and Cooley, and the lands sold to the railroad, at nearly $100,000 less than well-known and responsible parties bid in writing under the terms of the treaty. • • • The whole thing was a bare-faced swindle; first, upon the tribe, which knew nothing of the treaty which had been obtained from a few by fraud; and secondly, upon the United States, which lost fully $100,000 by the subsequent sale."

This is a revival of an old, stale charge made about a year since by this same correspondent in the same paper, which seems to be the receptacle of all of this writer's fabrications, and which was deemed by the friends of the parties referred to to

be so transparently false, and which was so flatly contradicted by the public records, as to need no formal refutation. The treaty referred to provided that the Missouri River Railroad Company, whose roads were located through these lands, where many of those Indians lived, might, within a given period after the publication of the treaty, purchase them at not less than two dollars and fifty cents per acre, adding the appraised value of improvements; and if not so purchased by said company, then, under certain restrictions, to be sold to the highest bidder. The company gave notice of acceptance, filed bond as provided by the treaty, and demanded that the contract should be closed insisting that it was entitled, within the period fixed by the treaty, to the *exclusive right* to purchase at the stipulated price. Secretary Harlan, however, held that the treaty was susceptible of a different construction, and kept the matter open for other bids until near the close of the period named in the treaty. No other bid being received, he notified the company that its bid had been accepted. But on the same day, and before the contract had been executed and delivered, General Thomas Ewing, Jr., the law partner of the incoming Secretary, (Mr. Browning,) called at the Department, and filed a bid, as he stated, in the interests of certain clients of his, proposing to purchase these lands at the rate of three dollars and one cent per acre. The Secretary, doubting whether this bid had been received in time, informed the parties that under the existing state of facts he thought it would be advisable to let the whole matter go over, to to adjusted by Secretary Browning, who would take possession of the office in a few days. On the following day, however, General Ewing presented to Mr. Harlan the following letter, withdrawing his bid:

WASHINGTON, August 30, 1866.
Hon. James Harlan, Secretary of the Interior:

Sir: When I made my bid yesterday for the Delaware lands in Kansas, I had not seen or heard of the bond filed by the Missouri River Railroad Company on the 27th inst., and their letter inclosing it; nor of your having stated orally that the bond was satisfactory, and their proposition to purchase was accepted; nor of your letter of yesterday, addressed to the company, then already signed and recorded. I had not, either, carefully considered the 7th article of the Delaware treaty Since then, however, these several matters have been considered by me, and I am led to believe that even if the contract should be awarded to me, I shall be compelled to test in the courts the claims of the company to the right of purchase of the lands.

I do not consider the lands a good purchase at my offer, with a clouded or embarrassed title, and therefore ask leave to withdraw my bid, and receive back the certificate of deposit accompanying it.
Very truly yours,
THOMAS EWING, JR.

The withdrawal by General Ewing of his bid raised the question of his right to do so. On consultation with William T. Otto, the Assistant Secretary, to whom Mr. Harlan usually referred legal questions, and the writer hereof, then the Chief Clerk of the Department, as well is others learned in the law, the Secretary was advised that General Ewing was entitled to withdraw his bid at any time but before acceptance, the correctness of which, we presume, no lawyer will doubt. This bid being withdrawn then, and there being no other offer, the contract was closed with the above-named company. An examination of the treaty will show that it is at least doubtful whether the company had not been made preferred purchasers within the period; in other words, whether the company did not possess *exclusive* right to purchase at the stipulated rate per acre during the period fixed in the treaty; and if the company was thus pre'erred, as its officers insisted, then Mr. Harlan committed a legal error in holding the sale open for other bids, after receiving notice of the company's acceptance—an error which delayed, instead of benefited, the railroad company. In this whole transaction it is clear from the testimony that Mr. Harlan acted with scrupulous care, and sought to make the most he could out of the lands for the benefit of the Indians.

That the treaty was fairly negotiated, and was fully understood by the Delaware Indians, is fully apparent from the following letter from Superintendent Murphy, addressed to the Secretary soon after this slander appeared in its first form, about a year ago.

WASHINGTON, D. C., February 23, 1869.
Hon. James Harlan, United States Senator

Sir: My attention having been called to a letter published in the Cincinnati *Gazette*, from a correspondent in this city, relative to the treaty negotiated with the Delaware Indians in 1866, in which, after stating that "William H. Watson, a clerk in the Indian Department, was appointed a commissioner to visit Kansas and conclude a treaty with the Delaware Indians," it goes on to state that "Mr. Watson went immediately to Kansas and called upon Thomas Murphy, superintendent of Indian affairs for that State, and showed him the treaty and letter of instructions Mr. Murphy was sick in bed, and not being able to attend to the matter, directed his clerk to act for him. Watson and this clerk then got together three chiefs and four other Indians as counselors, and having manipulated them properly, obtained their signatures to the treaty, &c."

As one of the commissioners whose name is attached to the Delaware treaty of 1866, I deem it due to myself to state the facts relative to the making of this treaty, and as you were my superior officer at that time, I deem it proper to make the statement to you

Mr. Watson. Agent Pratt, and myself, were appointed commissioners to negotiate the treaty referred to. On Mr. Watson's arrival at Leavenworth, Kansas, I met him there, and we proceeded direct to the Delaware agency; runners were sent out to inform the Indians, and the day following we counseled with them relative to the business that had brought us there. As is customary with Indian tribes, the Indians after consultation among themselves, directed their chiefs and head men to make the treaty. They performed this service The treaty was written out by the commissioners, and after being fully explained, was signed by them and *all* the chiefs and head men of the Delaware Nation I was not sick at that time; was present during the negotiating of the treaty. If there was any manipulating of the chiefs, I knew nothing about it. I do know that the treaty was satisfactory to the Delaware Indians at that time, and I have never heard one of them complain about any of its provisions since.

So much in regard to that portion of the letter in the *Gazette* which refers to myself in connection with this matter; and, I have no hesitation in saying in regard to the other statements in said letter impugning your motives and those of the then Commissioner of Indian Affairs, that as far as I have any knowledge, they are wholly without foundation in fact

Very respectfully, your obedient servant,
THOMAS MURPHY,
Superintendent of Indian Affairs.

If we admit that, by more skillful management these lands might have been sold for the price named in the bid put in, and afterwards withdrawn by General Ewing, still the *Gazette* correspondent's reckless disregard of truth, or his total ignorance of the subject, is perfectly patent. In his haste to gratify his hostility to Senator Harlan, and at the same time create a sensation, he did not stop to add up the figures. Secretary Browning reports, in the document to which we have referred, that there were 92 568 93-100 acres of these lands, the difference between the total value of which, at $2 50 and $3 01 per acre, would be less than $18,000, instead of $100,000, as alleged by the writer. That the ridiculous story about the supposed righteous indignation of a clerk in the Indian Bureau is false, is clear from a perusal of the treaty, from which it will be seen that the Commissioner of Indian Affairs had nothing whatever to do with the sale. As a matter of fact that officer never intermeddled with the subject. The treaty made it the duty of the Secretary to make the sale, and he did make it, without the aid of the Commissioner. The succeeding allegation that the United States lost $100,000 in this sale of these lands, is equally destitute of truth, and that it is so needs no other proof than a knowledge of the fact that these lands were the exclusive property of the Delaware Indians, and were sold for their benefit.

We have thus, at the risk of being tedious, carefully and minutely traversed every allegation of the *Gazette* correspondent, presenting the affidavits of responsible parties personally conversant with the facts to which they testify, with receipted bills, in denial of the charges made against the ex Secretary, after having personally examined the public records, laws, and treaties, and files of the Interior Department. From this statement the public, so far as it may feel any interest in the subject, may know the precise facts and the whole truth, and we doubt not that the judgment of our readers will coincide with our own when we state that this narration establishes that the charges made against Senator Harlan are utterly groundless, and that no reliance should be placed hereafter in the productions of this correspondent, whenever, at least, they are designed to affect the conduct or character of individuals. It is now said that he has announced on the streets, to his "cronies and sympathizers," his purpose to "write down Senator Harlan," as pure a public man as lives, and ruin him in the public estimation. What this high-toned gentleman and patriotic correspondent may be able to make up from discharged servants and dismissed department employes, who are not always free from vindictive feelings, and a disposition to avenge injuries, real or imaginary, or what the fruitful imagination of a sensational, reckless correspondent may invent, no one can divine or anticipate; but after this *expose* of his malicious and unwarranted assault upon Senator Harlan, to say nothing of his other attacks upon prominent Republican statesmen, by which his true character is made known to his employers, we shall be surprised if the columns of the Cincinnati *Gazette* are prostituted hereafter to the dissemination of his slanders.

To give a sort of color to his vile charges, the *Gazette* correspondent absurdly demands to be put to the proof of his allegations in a court of law—a demand, in itself, an insult to common sense.

He is believed to be totally irresponsible, and in eager pursuit of notoriety, doubtless holding that a notoriety for infamy is preferable to total obscurity. There are just such depraved minds in all professions, and unfortunately for the press, it is not exempt from the common lot. But if this were not so in this case—if this deliberate slanderer were able to respond in damages—what compensation would such a judgment be to a pure and upright statesman of honorable fame for the injuries inflicted on his good name; the only legacy, perhaps, which he will be able to bequeath to his children?

Having known Senator Harlan long and well and believing that he is pure in his public as in his private life, we have prepared this vindication of his character from the assaults of the *Gazette* correspondent, urged thereto by that sense of common justice which should animate every heart, and which will, sooner or later, prove every just man's sure vindication. To us it has been no pleasant task, for attacks of this character, when shown, as in this case, to be malicious and unfounded, bring discredit upon the press, and lessen the dignity of its members. And in vindicating the gentleman assailed, we vindicate the press itself. It would be terrible, indeed, if defamation of this character could not be exposed and refuted by the same method by which it is disseminated; and hence, duty, as well as justice, demanded its vindication at our hands.

W. PENN. CLARKE.

www.ingramcontent.com/pod-product-compliance
Lightning Source LLC
Chambersburg PA
CBHW031158090426
42738CB00008B/1390